THE

HANDBOOK

OF

Pirates

Terry Deary

tin Brown

D1053982

ASTIC

For Richard Smith with thanks and admiration. TD

Thanks Atholl. MB

Text copyright © 2006 by Terry Deary.
Illustrations copyright © 2006 by Martin Brown and Atholl McDonald.

All rights reserved. Published by Scholastic Inc. SCHOLASTIC, SCHOLASTIC NONFICTION, and associated logos are trademarks and/or registered trademarks of Scholastic Inc. First published in the UK in 2006 by Scholastic Ltd. as *Horrible Histories Handbooks: Pirates*.

ISBN-13: 978-0-545-03302-2
ISBN-10: 0-545-03302-0

12 11 10 9 8 7 6 5 4 3 2   07 08 09 10 11 12/0

Printed in the U.S.A.   23
This edition first printing, May 2007

Contents

Introduction

What do you call a person who takes you prisoner and feeds you rats, mice, and caterpillars?

A THUG?

What do you call a person who nails your feet to the deck of a ship and then beats you to death?

A BULLY?

What do you call a person who chops you into pieces and eats you?

A CANNIBAL?

There is one word for all of these vicious people ... **Pirates.**

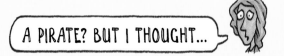

A PIRATE? BUT I THOUGHT...

Yes, it's shocking but true.

Forget the handsome young men, sailing the seven seas, digging up hidden treasure.

Forget the brave heroes swinging from masts to steal the gold from enemy galleons and laughing as they swish their swords.

Forget the fat, jolly storybook captain and his cheeky parrot with an eyepatch.

For this is a **HORRIBLE** history of pirates. And not only that, but it's everything you **DON'T** want to know about pirates in one handy little color handbook.

So, avast and belay you lubber, shiver your timbers and weigh your anchor, me hearties.[1]

Read this book and you may never plow the seven seas again!

1 No, I don't know what that means either. Just shout it as you swing from the ropes in the school gym.

Lousy legends and lies

You've seen the movies, you've read the books. Pirates are brave and handsome young men (and women) who wear gold earrings and shiny boots. They carry swords and pistols but never hurt anyone ... except the baddies.

Here are ten "facts" about storybook pirates. Can you say which of these are true?

If you think it may have happened say, **AYE, JIM LAD!**

 If you think it was a lie then say,

NEVER, ME HEARTIES.

1. Pirates were gentlemen thieves.

Answer: "Aye, Jim lad!" Blackbeard was thought to be a "learned" man born into a well-to-do family. Henry Morgan was made "Sir Henry" by King Charles II and went on to be governor of Jamaica. But some were not even men! Mary Read and Anne Bonney were a couple of tough women who swashed and buckled alongside the men.

2. Pirates carried parrots.

Answer: "Aye, Jim lad!" The parrots were captured in South America and carried back home. But they weren't just cute pets – they could be sold for good money in Europe. Pretty Polly made a pretty penny.

3. Pirates stole Spanish gold and jewels.

Answer: "Aye, Jim lad!" But the Spanish ships became too big and too well-armed. Pirates turned to stealing things they could sell – sugar and cloth were popular. Slaves made a good price. Never mind the misery.

4. Pirates made maps of buried treasure.

Answer: "Never, me hearties." They shared the money and spent it quickly. There was no point in burying it. Captain Kidd was supposed to have buried treasure, but no one has ever found it. It's a crazy thing to do with your loot when you think about it. The only pirates who buried their loot were the ones being chased by the navy. They would hide it for a couple of days till it was safe to move on.

5. Pirates marooned shipmates on desert islands.

Answer: "Aye, Jim lad!" It was a punishment for a pirate who broke the rules. Believe it or not, pirates did have a set of rules – just like school rules! The rules even said what time you had to put your lights out and go to bed!

6. Pirates had wooden legs and eyepatches.

Answer: "Aye, Jim lad!" Cannon shots could mangle legs and smash faces. A saw would take off a crushed leg and there was always wood to make a handy new stump – if stinking gangrene in the wound didn't kill you first.

TREASURE!
I'M RICH!
MAROONED...
BUT RICH!

7. Pirates flew skull-and-crossbones flags.

Answer: "Aye, Jim lad!" But other flags had bleeding hearts or daggers or whole skeletons on them. A lot of "pirate" flags may have been invented long after the pirates were dead.

8. Pirates made enemies walk the plank.

Answer: "Never, me hearties." That was just for stories. Pirates never wasted their time. If they wanted enemies dead they just chopped them to pieces and fed them to the sharks. Chinese pirates may have made victims walk the plank – and one writer said Black Bart did it in the Caribbean. But that's probably not true. It may be true that they threw a victim into the sea and called out …

YOU'RE FREE TO WALK HOME. HAH!

NO ONE LIKES A SMARTY PANTS

9. Pirates sent their victims a black spot to show they were coming to get them.

Answer: "Aye, Jim lad!" A circle of paper was cut out and covered in black ink. The circle was then sent to someone they planned to kill. It meant, "We are going to kill you." If the victim waited they were killed – and if they tried to run they were killed. The black-spot warning added to their terror before they died.

hug and kisses
Jim

10. Pirates wore fine clothes, black beards, and curly wigs.

Answer: "Aye, Jim lad!" They liked to steal fine clothes from their victims and, if they fit, they wore them. But people like Blackbeard grew a long tangled beard just to look scary. It looked less scary when his head was lopped off in a fight with the British Navy.

Nasty names

Not all robbers who took to the seas were known as pirates. But if someone is nailing your foot to the deck you don't want to upset him and call him by the wrong name. So here are the correct names.

Pirate

(also spelled pyrate, pyrat, or pirat)
Did you know, the word "Peirato" was first used about 140 BC by the Greek writer Polybius? Another Greek writer, Plutarch (around 100 AD), said …

Pirates are people who attack not only ships but seaports too.

Viking

These nasty Norsemen from Denmark, Norway, and Sweden liked battering poor little monks and flattening farmers from the 700s to the 1000s. But they also attacked ships at sea. Some history books say the word "Viking" is a Norse word for pirate. But why would they call themselves "pirates"? It may come from the Vikings' own word for "creek," where the Vikings launched their boats, or it may come from the English word that means "trader." No one will ever be sure.

Buccaneer

These pirates from the 1600s and 1700s killed wild cows in the Caribbean. They then cooked them over a sort of barbecue – the French word for a man with a barbecue is "boucanier" – so these barbecue bandits were hot stuff. The buccaneers also called themselves "Brothers of the Coast."

ARE YOU A BROTHER OF THE COAST?

I SHORE AM! SHORE! GEDDIT? I'M A SIBLING OF THE SAND, TWIN OF THE TIDE, KIN OF THE CLIFF, BRO OF THE BEACH!

A SIMPLE "YES" WOULD HAVE DONE

Corsair

Another French word. This one means a "chaser." So watch out or they'll chase YOU and rob you. Usually corsair was the name for pirates who robbed people in the Mediterranean Sea.

Privateer

These were pirates who went into "private" business. The English kings and queens of the 1600s couldn't afford to build a navy to fight the Spanish, so they said to the "private-eers" ...

GO OFF AND ATTACK THE SPANISH SHIPS – GIVE ME A SHARE OF THE LOOT AND WE BOTH GET RICH

A PRIVATE PIRATE WITH PROPER PERMISSION TO PEDDLE PAIN AND PANIC IN THE PACIFIC?

YOU COULD SAY THAT, BUT I'D RATHER YOU DIDN'T

Barbary pirate

These foul fellers attacked ships off the Barbary Coast – that is, North Africa. Do not mix Barbary pirates up with the cheerful chaps who cut corsair hair – they are pirate barbers. From 1569 to 1616, nearly five hundred English ships were captured by the Barbary pirates. They would send the fit English sailors to the slave markets. The unfit would have their throats slit. (That saved the trouble of feeding them.)

Sea rover

A polite word for a pirate. Call him this if he has a cutlass to your throat. Sea king is an even MORE polite word for a pirate – makes him sound like some fancy hero. Really he's see-king to rob you.

ROVER IS A DOG'S NAME

Marooner

Marooner comes from the Spanish word "cimarrona" and means a "runaway." These men were either runaway slaves or Spanish sailors who ran away from the cruel life on their treasure ships – they slaved away on the ships but didn't get a share of the treasure. No wonder they ran away. In time the word "marooning" was used to mean leaving a victim on a deserted island – this is not the same as the purple color known as maroon. And it has nothing at all to do with this awful joke …

I SAY! I SAY! I SAY! A SHIP FULL OF RED PAINT CRASHED INTO A SHIP FULL OF BLUE PAINT AND THEY SANK. THE CREW WERE MAROONED!

Freebooter

A Dutch word for thieves who roam around (freely) looking for loot (booty). Do not mix him up with a soccer star who has an extra leg:

FREEBOOTER

THREE-BOOTER

Filibuster

Spanish word for a pirate. Useful if you are attacked while on vacation.

HAND OVER YOUR INNER TUBE

FILIBUSTER!

Top ten putrid pirates

Here's a quick guide to the pirates you would NOT want to see at sea or cross cutlasses with in a cabin.

Their horrors have been scored with skulls! A one-skull pirate is nasty – but a five-skull pirate is more deadly than a crocodile with a toothache.

1. Blackbeard (Edward Teach, 1680–1718)

• He sometimes killed his own crew for sport. He shot his mate Israel Hands in the knee and crippled him for life, just for fun.

• He wore braids in his beard and hair so it looked like snakes were crawling over his face and head. He also twisted smoking rope into the braids to add to his terrifying looks.

• He was so strong he could split a man from his head to his waist with one blow from his cutlass.

Skull Score: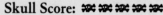

I'M OFF

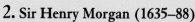

2. Sir Henry Morgan (1635–88)

• This Welshman started off as a privateer, attacking the Spanish for King Charles. He did such a good job Charles made him governor of Jamaica.

• Morgan was a good soldier but a hopeless sailor. He wrecked one ship by sailing it onto rocks. He had to cling to a rock and wait to be rescued. Embarrassing.

• Another of his ships blew up when some drunken sailors knocked a candle over in the gunpowder store. Morgan lived – 250 of his crew died.

Skull Score: ✺✺ ✺✺

3. Coxinga (1624–62)

• Coxinga was the son of China's richest smuggler. He fought to defend his emperor and built a navy of 3,000 ships and 250,000 fighting men. When the emperor was finally defeated Coxinga turned to piracy.

• He couldn't return to China so he decided to drive out the Dutch traders on Taiwan Island. The Dutch refused to surrender. Coxinga had the Dutch captives divided into groups of about 30 and sent to villages around his camp. There they were dragged out, killed, and thrown into burial pits.

• Coxinga went mad and started screaming, "Take those headless bodies out of my bedroom!" There was nothing there.

Skull Score: ✺✺ ✺✺ ✺✺

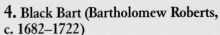

4. Black Bart (Bartholomew Roberts, c. 1682–1722)

• Bart started his life at sea working on a slave ship. Then a pirate captured him and made Bart a slave. The hard-working Welshman earned his freedom and in time became captain of his own ship. Bart once captured a ship and asked the captain to pay if he wanted to go free. The captain refused, so Bart set his ship on fire. It didn't bother Bart that there were eighty slaves on board.

• Black Bart was an odd pirate because he didn't drink – he had a clear head to plan his clever attacks. He also hated gambling and smoking on his ship.

• Bart found time to preach to his crew on Sundays. His rule was "Never attack on a Sunday, it is the Lord's Day."

Skull Score: ☠☠ ☠☠ ☠☠

5. Ned Low (died c. 1724)

• This American pickpocket turned to pirating. He refused to have married men on his crew. He didn't want men running home to their wives. If a prisoner was married, then he couldn't turn pirate – Low shot him in the head.

• Low captured the Spanish galleon *Montcova* and killed 53 Spanish captives with his cutlass. He made one Spanish prisoner eat the heart of his friend, then he killed him. He burned a French cook alive. Low told him …

YOU ARE A GREASY FELLOW SO YOU'LL FRY WELL

• His own crew set him adrift in a small boat. A French ship rescued him. When they found out who he was, they hanged him.

Skull Score: ✖✖ ✖✖ ✖✖ ✖✖ ✖✖

6. Jeanne de Clisson (c. 1300s)

• In 1313 Jeanne's husband, Olivier de Clisson, was executed on the orders of Philip the Fair, King of France. Jeanne decided he was Philip the Un-fair and decided to get revenge. First she sold off all her lands to raise money, then she bought three warships; they were painted black and had red sails. Admiral Jeanne began destroying Philip's ships and murdering their crews … but she always left two or three alive to carry the story back to the King. After all, that was part of the fun!

• Philip died – which could have spoiled Jeanne's fun, but she decided to continue her revenge on his sons as they took the French throne. After 13 bloody years the last son of Philip died and Jeanne retired.

• It was said that she enjoyed capturing ships with French noblemen on board. Then she would personally chop off their heads with her axe. Her gray ghost still walks the walls of Clisson Castle – don't go there if your name is Philip!

Skull Score: ✖✖ ✖✖ ✖✖ ✖✖

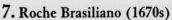

7. Roche Brasiliano (1670s)

• This Dutch buccaneer lived in Brazil, then turned up in Jamaica in the 1670s to do some pirating.

• Brasiliano was a drunkard famous for his hatred of the Spanish. He would get drunk and run down the street beating anyone who got in his way.

• He soon became a pirate captain and brought terror to Spanish shipping. His nastiest trick was to capture a Spaniard, tie him to a pole, and roast him alive over a fire.

Skull Score: ✖✖ ✖✖ ✖✖ ✖✖

8. Juan Corso (1680s)

• The Spanish were not just victims of piracy. Some Spaniards, like Juan Corso, became pirates themselves – and cruel ones, too.

• Corso became a Spanish privateer with orders to destroy the English in Jamaica. He gathered a crew of killers who robbed and murdered without pity.

• Once, one of Corso's crew fell sick. He was not able to row Corso's boat. He was useless ... so Corso cut off his head.

Skull Score: ✖✖ ✖✖ ✖✖

9. Lady Mary Killigrew (1580s)

• This cutthroat woman was the wife of Sir John Killigrew and they lived in Cornwall. She went on many pirating cruises along the English coast and was happy to slash and chop with her own sword. In 1583 a German merchant ship was robbed and she rowed away with jewels, silver, and pieces of eight. After killing the crew, of course.

• In the same year a Spanish merchant ship was driven into Falmouth by storms. Lady Killigrew led a boarding party onto the vessel, killed the crew, and stole the cargo.

• Queen Elizabeth I heard about the attack and was furious. Lady Killigrew was tried and sentenced to be hanged along with her crew. But at the last minute the Queen, who liked Lady Killigrew, changed her mind and gave her a long jail sentence instead.

Skull Score: 🕱 🕱 🕱 🕱

10. François l'Olonoise (1660s)

• L'Olonoise, a French pirate, brought terror to the coast of South America ... He tortured his prisoners and became famous as the cruelest of all pirates.

• His nastiest habit was cutting prisoners to bits when he lost his temper. Then he would cut out their tongues. Once he cut out a prisoner's heart and started chewing it while asking him questions.

• L'Olonoise was wrecked on the island of Las Pertas. He was found by local natives and was murdered in a horrible way. Served him right.

Skull Score: ✗✗ ✗✗ ✗✗ ✗✗ ✗✗

Perilous pirate timeline

To give you a rough idea of who was doing what and when, here is a quick timeline...

Around 1100 BC The first pirates roam the Mediterranean seas.

230 BC Queen Teuta of Illyria (that's Albania today) is fed up with the Greeks settling on the coast of her country. She hasn't the forces to drive them out of their towns, so she turns pirate to sink them at sea. But when she tries to be ruthless with Roman ships she is defeated.

Vikings cross the North Sea and slaughter monks.

AD 793 It's the start of the Viking age. They will spill blood on land and sea for more than three hundred years.

AD 401 St. Patrick (AD 385–461) was a British boy who was taught the Bible by his dad. When St. Pat was sixteen he was captured by pirates and sold as a slave in Ireland. After six years he

escaped to Gaul (now France) and became a monk. He then went BACK to Ireland and converted the Irish to Christianity. If the pirates hadn't sent him to Ireland he might never have become their greatest saint. Don't be surprised. Scramble the letters of "pirates" and you get "a priest."

☠ DID YOU KNOW…? ☠

Lancelot Blackburne was a priest in the Caribbean but found the pay was poor, so he joined a pirate ship and attacked Spanish galleons. He returned to England to work as a priest. Was he hanged for piracy? No. He was made Archbishop of York.

1492 Christopher Columbus discovers the West Indies and finds that the Arawak Indians make great slaves. He starts the slave trade that has traders crossing the Atlantic to make their fortunes – and pirates to steal it.

1500s The Barbarossa brothers, Aruj and Kheir-ed-din, roam the Mediterranean. The name means "Red beard," which is better than being called "Green beard." These corsairs were feared throughout the

Mediterranean for their vicious attacks on Christian ships and towns.

1603 England stops allowing her "privateers" to attack foreign ships, but the English sailors carry on the raids anyway against the law. These are the days of the buccaneers in the Caribbean.

WE'RE ILLEGAL CRIMINALS NOW

1618 There are now about 5,000 pirates at sea – mostly in the Caribbean. There's a great trade there in slaves and sugar plus lots of lovely hiding places thousands of miles from the nasty navies. A pirate paradise in fact.

NO NAVIES? NAY NIGH NOR NEAR

1697 Treaty of Ryswick. Spain, France, Holland, and England agree to stop privateers raiding each other's ships. Pirates can no longer say, "I was fighting for my country," and get away with it. A caught pirate is a dead pirate from now on. Just to prove it the English hang Captain Kidd in 1701.

NO KIDD-ING

1775 The Americans are in revolt against Britain. American ships start to attack and rob British ships. John Paul Jones makes a daring raid on Britain and becomes an American hero. The Brits just see him as a pirate.

dashing   bashing

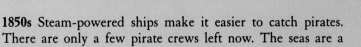

1850s Steam-powered ships make it easier to catch pirates. There are only a few pirate crews left now. The seas are a bit safer.

Lousy loot

If you were a pirate, what on earth would you steal? At sea there are no cars or cell phones, no jewelry shops or cash machines. Here are a few top tips on what to take and what not...

Pieces of eight

Pieces of eight were Spanish silver dollars. The little Spanish coins were called "reals" – put EIGHT reals together and you got one "piece of eight." If you had SIXTEEN pieces of eight they were worth one "doubloon" – that was a gold coin. You could spend these coins all over the world.

Jewelry

If the ship had passengers, then you could rob them of their rings and watches. Blackbeard liked to save time with this hand-chopping trick:

IF YOU CAN'T GET A RING OFF THEN CHOP OFF THE FINGER

IF THERE ARE A FEW RINGS AND YOU'RE IN A REAL HURRY, CHOP OFF THE HAND AND SLIDE THEM OFF LATER

Wine

Pirates liked a drink … a lot of drink. Some drank themselves to death. So if they could bag a barrel without paying, they would. Otherwise they'd have to go to an inn. Then there would be the excuse to tell the joke …

A PIRATE WALKS INTO A BAR. "OUCH!" HE SAID.

IT WAS AN IRON BAR!

Cloth

Any sort of cloth would be easy to sell, but silk from China was best of all. By 1623 the Chinese were sick of Dutch pirates stealing their silk. They pretended to be friendly with Dutch Captain Franszoon and gave him beer … it was poisoned. Franszoon spat it out. So they tried to ram him with fire ships – blazing boats sent to ram Franszoon's ships and set them alight. They missed Franszoon but hit his partner's ship. It blew up in a fireball. The Dutch report said …

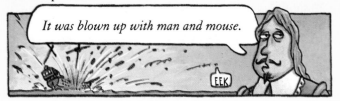

It was blown up with man and mouse.

EEK

Maps

Maps were very valuable. You couldn't just go into a shop and buy one. If you find a trader's maps you can learn all about the trade routes. Then you can lay traps for other ships.

In 1680 Captain Bartholomew Sharp captured Spanish treasure near Chile. The Spanish demanded that King Charles II of England punish the pirate when he went back to England. But part of Bart's treasure was a book of sea maps and plans of the South Seas. These were so important that King Charles II gave them a free pardon instead!

Sugar

Sugar was one of the most precious things you could have in England in the 1700s. Thousands of slaves were captured just to grow and harvest sugar in the Caribbean. Growing sugar was hard work. Much easier to let the slaves do all the work, then steal the sugar planters' cargo when they sent it across to England.

Slaves

Slave ships took Africans to America and sold them to work in the fields. It was easy to attack a slave ship and steal the Africans. But one of the oddest raids was led by the Dutch pirate Jan Jansz. He led a crew of Barbary pirates to Iceland. They landed, snatched a village full of Iceland peasants, and sold them as slaves.

WHY SHOULD I BUY A SLAVE FROM ICELAND?

THEY'RE REALLY COOL!

Cattle

Captain Basil Hood was arrested off the coast of Central America in 1713 for being a pirate. But the English Navy officers wondered what the foul smell was. It seems he had the ship full of live cattle, not treasure. But, worse, the cattle were ill. The American Indians called the cattle illness "a volcano of vomit" and that's what the cattle were spewing out. The naval officers let Hood go and left his ship very quickly.

THE HULL IS ALIVE WITH THE SOUND OF MOO-SICK

Medicine

Sick sailors were no use to a pirate captain. Medicine was a valuable prize. Once Blackbeard held a town for ransom. He said he'd kill his captives if they didn't send him a chest full of medicine. He got his precious pills and potions.

Fish

Not many pirates were able to rob Spanish galleons and treasure ships loaded with gold. Pirates like Jack Rackham spent a lot of time attacking little fishing boats in the Caribbean. Why? Because they were hungry and not powerful enough to attack bigger ships.

Wicked weapons

If you want to be a pirate you need to have plenty of weapons. You will want to stab, shoot, smash down doors, chop through ropes, and burn sails.

Here are some usual – and unusual – weapons for you to wear.

Cutlass

Why did pirates like the curvy cutlass sword? Because there were lots of ropes on a sailing ship. The curved sword didn't get tangled in the ropes. Unless you used it the wrong way around, of course …

Brass knife

Salty water makes iron and steel rot and rust. A brass knife would stay sharp. It was usually short and sharp for cutting and stabbing. (It is also useful for picking your teeth if you've forgotten to pack your corsair toothbrush. Just don't use it to pick your nose.)

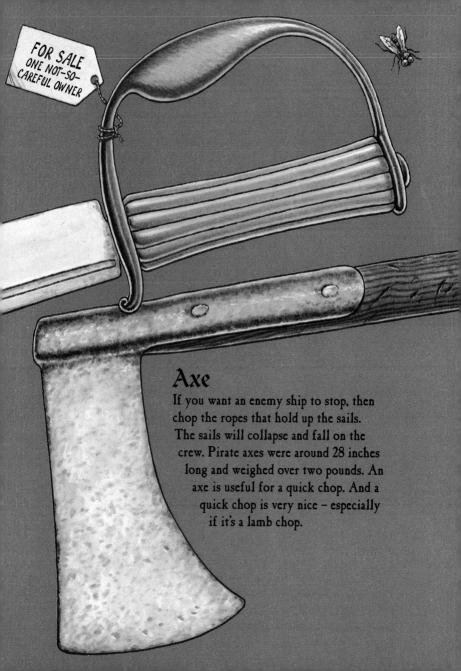

FOR SALE
ONE NOT-SO-
CAREFUL OWNER

Axe

If you want an enemy ship to stop, then chop the ropes that hold up the sails. The sails will collapse and fall on the crew. Pirate axes were around 28 inches long and weighed over two pounds. An axe is useful for a quick chop. And a quick chop is very nice – especially if it's a lamb chop.

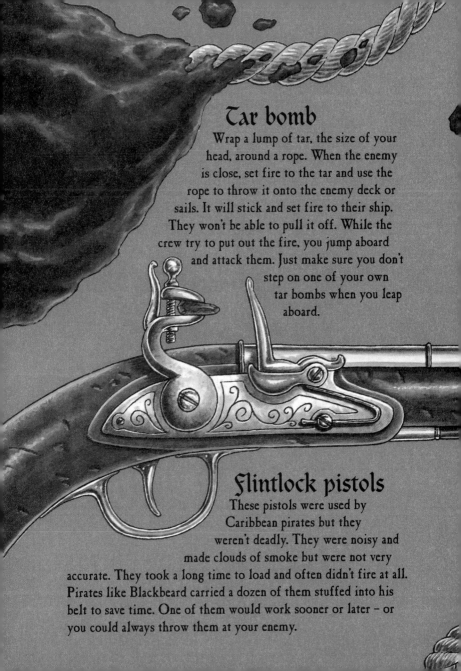

Tar bomb

Wrap a lump of tar, the size of your head, around a rope. When the enemy is close, set fire to the tar and use the rope to throw it onto the enemy deck or sails. It will stick and set fire to their ship. They won't be able to pull it off. While the crew try to put out the fire, you jump aboard and attack them. Just make sure you don't step on one of your own tar bombs when you leap aboard.

Flintlock pistols

These pistols were used by Caribbean pirates but they weren't deadly. They were noisy and made clouds of smoke but were not very accurate. They took a long time to load and often didn't fire at all. Pirates like Blackbeard carried a dozen of them stuffed into his belt to save time. One of them would work sooner or later – or you could always throw them at your enemy.

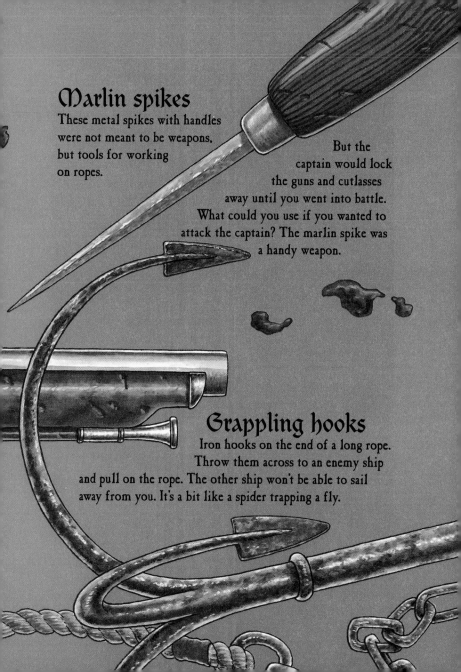

Marlin spikes

These metal spikes with handles were not meant to be weapons, but tools for working on ropes.

But the captain would lock the guns and cutlasses away until you went into battle. What could you use if you wanted to attack the captain? The marlin spike was a handy weapon.

Grappling hooks

Iron hooks on the end of a long rope. Throw them across to an enemy ship and pull on the rope. The other ship won't be able to sail away from you. It's a bit like a spider trapping a fly.

Buccaneer knives

Buccaneers in the Caribbean enjoyed hunting wild pigs or boars. They were expert shots, but DIDN'T use their guns to kill the pigs. They enjoyed the "sport" of running after the boar and chopping it down with their long sharp knives. Each buccaneer had at least two large knives. These knives were shorter than a cutlass. The aim was to slice the back legs of the pig so it couldn't run. They would then jump it from behind and slit its throat.

Duck's foot

If you want to shoot someone use a duck's foot. This was a pistol with FOUR barrels. You could fire all four at the same time so you were sure to hit something. The barrels were joined together and looked a little like a duck's foot. You'd be quackers not to use one!

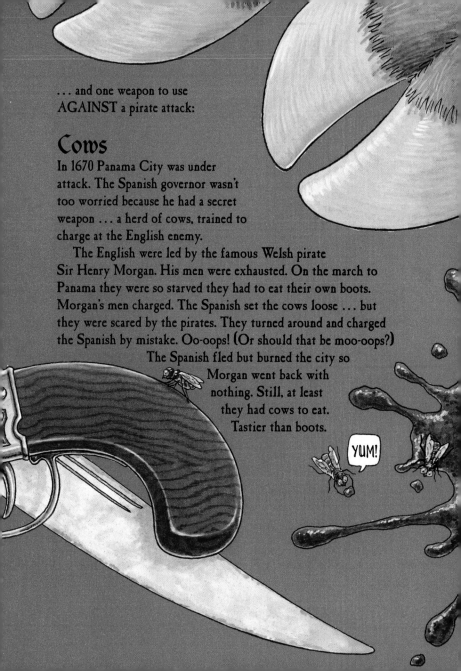

... and one weapon to use
AGAINST a pirate attack:

Cows

In 1670 Panama City was under
attack. The Spanish governor wasn't
too worried because he had a secret
weapon ... a herd of cows, trained to
charge at the English enemy.

The English were led by the famous Welsh pirate
Sir Henry Morgan. His men were exhausted. On the march to
Panama they were so starved they had to eat their own boots.
Morgan's men charged. The Spanish set the cows loose ... but
they were scared by the pirates. They turned around and charged
the Spanish by mistake. Oo-oops! (Or should that be moo-oops?)
The Spanish fled but burned the city so
Morgan went back with
nothing. Still, at least
they had cows to eat.
Tastier than boots.

YUM!

☠ DID YOU KNOW…? ☠

If you were a trader and afraid of pirates, how could you defend your ship? Put cannon on board? But it was hard to find good gunners – they were either in the navy or on pirate ships. And a cannon is no good without a gunner. So some shipowners painted pictures of cannon on the sides of their ships and hoped they would scare the pirates away.

TERRIBLE TACTICS

You can't just jump on a ship and sail off looking for other ships to attack. Pirates had special ways of doing things – tactics.

RANSOM A SHIP

Capture a ship and sell it back to the owner. That saves you taking the captured ships to port, selling the treasure, and killing the crew.

Black Bart, a Welshman, was a good sailor and fighter. He terrorized the ships in the Caribbean and off the Guinea coast. In one raid he captured eleven ships and sold ten back to their owners.

FAKE FEMALES

The easiest way to capture a ship is to get yourself invited on board. Once you are on the deck, you pull out your weapons and surprise the crew.

But how do you trick the victims? After all, no one would invite a pirate on board their ship.

A painter called Auguste Francois Biard painted a picture of pirates taking a ship. The pirates are all dressed as women. We don't know if it really happened, but if it did, it was crafty.

HOW'S ME LIPPY?

ARRR! THAT BE FINE. 'TIS YOUR EYELINER THAT'S A MESS

HOAX HELP

If you see a rich ship then don't attack it. Put up a signal flag that means, "Help!" Every ship has to go to the rescue of a ship in trouble. It's the rule of the seas. So the treasure ship sails towards the pirate ship. When the two are side by side the "troubled" pirate suddenly springs to life and attacks. Sneaky.

FIRE CANNON

Pirate ships didn't want to sink other ships – they wanted to rob them. But sometimes they would shoot to smash the masts – or just to scare their victims into giving up.

But firing a cannon wasn't an easy job. The master gunner would have to call out these orders ... in the right order!

"Cast off the tackles and breechings."

"Seize the breechings."

"Unstop the touchhole."

"Ram home wad and cartridge."

"Shoot the gunwad."

"Run out the gun."

"Lay down handspikes and crows."

"Point your gun."

"Fire!"

Then start all over again for the next shot.

Really cruel pirates would fire "bar" shot or "chain" shot – cannonballs that split open when they landed and scattered deadly splinters or chains all over the deck. They could tear down a mast – and they could also tear a man to shreds.

40

GHOST SHIP

Around 1720 Anne Bonney, the pirate queen, saw a merchant ship coming her way. She got her men to cover themselves in red paint and lie on the deck of her ship. It looked as if they were covered in blood after a massacre.

When a terrified crew from a merchant ship came aboard to bury the corpses, the "dead" men leaped into life and killed them. Red paint and real blood flooded the deck. Yeuch.

FLY THE FLAG

Pirate ships looked a lot like other ships ... until they raised the "Jolly Roger" flag with its skull and crossbones (see page 69).

So some crafty pirates would raise a friendly flag and let their prize come close. When the other ship was in reach, the pirates suddenly switched flags to the pirate flag and attacked.

But SOMETIMES they fell into their own trap. Black Bart was being hunted by the English Navy. He was happy to see a ship with a French flag and sailed up to it. Suddenly the French flag was cut down and the English flag took its place.

The "French" ship was an English Navy ship. Black Bart found out too late. Within minutes he was dead.

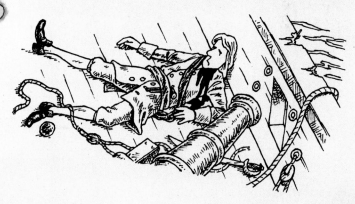

BRUTAL BATTLES

In a sea battle the Vikings would try to ram their enemies' boats head-on. When the boats collided, they would jump across and fight until one side won or they were exhausted. Sometimes they had to stop when the dead bodies were piled too high. When ships started to use cannon they were usually along the side of the deck. So pirates knew it was best to attack ships from the back.

TAKE THE MONEY AND RUN

Roman rebel Spartacus (who died in 71 BC) was in trouble and wanted to escape to Sicily. He made a deal with a pirate fleet — they would take Spartacus and his men to safety, and Spartacus would pay them.

Spartacus paid them. The pirates sailed off without him.

(Don't feel too sorry for Spartacus the sap. He once crucified 300 Roman soldiers in revenge for the death of his friend.)

☠ DID YOU KNOW…? ☠

Pirate ships did NOT attack navy ships. They might lose the battle. They were cowards and bullies who attacked trading ships that had no guns or fighting men on board.

Wicked women pirates

People like unusual stories. The idea of women pirates is a bit odd. There are many foul females in pirate legend ... the trouble is many of them are just fibs about females. You need a helpful look at the true and the terrible rumors that have been spread. Can you spot the real stories from the ones that are as false as a wooden leg?

Queen Teuta of the Illyrians

This queen of Illyria (Albania today) reigned between 231 and 228 BC. She set out to attack cities in the Mediterranean. On the way they came across some Roman traders and robbed them. Queen Teuta liked this idea – her ships took up piracy.

The Romans sent two messengers to warn her to stop. That upset Teuta and she had the messengers murdered.

That made the Romans really mad. They invaded Illyria and defeated her.

Sadie the Goat

I'M A BUTTING BUCCANEER!

Sadie worked as a mugger in New York around 1850. She would head-butt her victim in the stomach then rob him. That's how she got her name "the Goat." The streets of New York were too tough for her: When her ear was bitten off in a fight she left to be a pirate. She collected her chewed-off ear and wore it on a chain around her neck. She sailed around the coast near New York attacking ships.

Sadie read pirate books and tried to behave like the pirates of the Caribbean … she even made victims walk the plank (which was just a storybook torture until then).

Her crew of thugs made very little money and they went back to the slums of New York.

Granuaile

IT'S A CREW CUT

Grace O'Malley (1530–1603) led a fleet of Irish raiders who attacked English ships around 1577. She was known as Granuaile because she cropped her hair very short and Granuaile means "Bald" in Irish.

In 1593 she was arrested and her ships were taken away from her. She was furious, so she went to Queen Elizabeth I to complain. Queen Bess gave Granuaile money so she could give up the pirate life.

Two hundred years after she died a Scottish farmer sent a ship to western Ireland to rob old cemeteries. He stole the bones to grind and use as fertilizer. Unfortunately his robbers stole Grace's skull, and her angry spirit was avenged in a strange way. One of her teeth found its way into a turnip which the thieving Scottish farmer ate and choked on!

Mary Read

Mary's mother disguised her as a boy to get her a job as a manservant. Mary ran off to join the French army.

She was captured by a pirate crew with a woman pirate, Anne Bonney – they became friends and Mary decided to join them. When one of her boyfriends got into a duel she took his place … and won.

She was captured and sent to prison. She was not hanged but in 1721 died of fever in the filthy cell.

Anne Bonney

Anne Bonney (1700–22) was the girlfriend of pirate Jack Rackham. She decided to join his pirate crew and dressed herself as a man.

When the navy came to get Jack he gave up without a fight. The only ones fighting were Anne and her friend, Mary Read.

Anne was disgusted with Jack and his men. She was happy to watch him hang, and said …

If you would have fought like a man you needn't die like a dog.

Cutlass Liz

Elizabeth Stirland was born in Devon in 1577 and sailed to America to start a new life. But native American Indians wiped out her colony – she only escaped by stabbing her guard.

She returned to England but got bored. She went back to sea as a pirate, dressed as a man, and robbed Spanish ships of their fortune. She earned the name "Cutlass Liz" because she enjoyed cutting men's throats with her cutlass.

She was betrayed by a Spaniard. As she was led out to execution she managed to kill the traitor with a hidden knife.

Gunpowder Gertie

PIRATING IS A BLAST

In 1898 Gertrude Stubbs was sacked from her job on a coal ship. She took her revenge by stealing a police boat and using it to rob ships near Whitby (north Yorkshire, England). One of her crew was captured and he said, "I'll tell you all about Gertie if you set me free." He betrayed her.

Gertie was arrested and died of a fever in jail. Her treasure was never discovered.

Maria Cobham

She sailed the Atlantic with her pirate husband in the 1700s. A writer said, "Murder for Maria was a pleasure and a sport."

She killed a navy officer, stripped off his uniform, and wore it for her pirate raids.

She once had three prisoners lined up on deck and used them for shooting practice. She retired to France with her husband but her past haunted her horribly. She took a lonely walk along the cliffs, drank poison, and threw herself in the sea.

Charlotte de Berry

Charlotte was born in England in 1636. When she grew up she fell in love with a sailor. When the Royal Navy ordered him to sea, she donned male clothes and joined him on board his ship as his brother.

Sometime after the navy ship left

England, pirates attacked it. The pirate captain discovered Charlotte was a woman, but she fought a duel with him and lopped off his head. The pirates made Charlotte their new captain.

She was more cruel than any pirate king. One story said she had sewn shut a captain's mouth. In her final battle Charlotte's husband was killed. She won the battle ... then leaped overboard to join her dead husband.

Alwilda

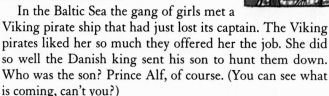

Alwilda was a Viking princess around AD 850. Her father said, "You must marry Prince Alf of Denmark." Alwilda had never met Alf and didn't like the sound of him. She dressed as a man and ran off to sea with a few friends.

In the Baltic Sea the gang of girls met a Viking pirate ship that had just lost its captain. The Viking pirates liked her so much they offered her the job. She did so well the Danish king sent his son to hunt them down. Who was the son? Prince Alf, of course. (You can see what is coming, can't you?)

Alf tracked down Alwida's pirates and attacked. He fought so bravely Alwilda fell in love with him at once. She surrendered ... and married him.

Did you separate the fiction from the truth? Liz, Gertie, Maria, Charlotte, and Alwilda were all fiction.

Here are the facts:

• The story of Cutlass Liz is a local legend, BUT ... the real Elizabeth Stirland never left Devon. Anyway, people of those days didn't much use the word "cutlass" or "Liz" – they called pirate swords "hangers" and the short name for "Elizabeth" was

"Bess" … if she'd really been a pirate, she'd have been Hanger Bess!

• Gertie's story was made up by a teacher who told it to her class. She sent it to a newspaper as an April fool joke. A lot of people believe it and say there really WAS a Gunpowder Gertie. There wasn't.

• Maria Cobham and her husband were probably completely made up.

• Charlotte's story was first printed in 1836. Many people believe it. Yet it is too crazy to be true.

• Alwilda's story was probably half truth, half legend.

Cutthroat cruelties

Pirates were tough on their enemies ... and tough on their friends. Many sailors worked on trading ships and learned to hate the cruel captains. When a sailor turned to piracy, he would make sure the trader captain suffered most of all. They would sometimes question the captured crew ...

IS YOUR CAPTAIN KIND TO YOU?

If the answer was "No" then the captain could die.

Pirate Phillip Lyne said in 1726 that he had murdered 37 captains. That was not the only cruelty that went on at sea ...

Moses' Law

The Bible said that 40 lashes of a whip would kill a man. If a pirate captain wanted to punish a man – but not kill him – he would order 39 lashes. The truth is a weak man could easily die from 20 lashes. There are also reports of sailors being lashed 100 times and living.

The Romans also used the 39-lash rule. But their whips had 12 strands and lead weights at the end, or even hooks. It tore the skin and flesh off the back. The sailors' "cat-o'-nine-tails" whips had nine strands with knots at the end.

The trouble is the "cat" would be soaked in the stale blood of the last victim. The germs would get into the next man's wounds. If the whipping didn't kill you, the blood poisoning might.

Marooning

A pirate killer or a pirate who stole from his mates could be marooned – that is, dropped off on a deserted island with a bottle of rum, a pistol, and some gunpowder.

Better than death?

No. It was worse. It was a slow death. It was never an island with water and fruit, animals to shoot and eat, wood to burn. Just rock or sand. The pirate would die slowly … or he could use the pistol to shoot himself.

Keelhauling

The bottom of a wooden ship – the "keel"[2] – soon had a crust of shellfish stuck to it. This slowed the ship down.

2 "What was the keel?" I hear you cry. It was a long wooden spar that ran down the center of the hull for the whole length of the ship.

The ship had to be run up onto a beach so the shells could be scraped off. But the rough sides could also be used to punish a sailor. A rope was fastened to the victim's feet and hands. He was dragged across the rough bottom of the ship and up the other side. Sometimes this would be done at sea so the sailor couldn't breathe as he was dragged under.

Shooting

Shooting a pirate was quick and simple. It taught the crew a lesson.

In the 1740s pirate Captain Daniel kidnapped a priest and forced him to have a Christian service on his ship. One of the pirate crew thought it was a joke. He made a very rude sign to the priest. Captain Daniel drew his pistol and shot the man dead.

Chinese choppers
Some Chinese pirates were very cruel. Captives were crushed into tiny cabins then fed on rats, mice, and caterpillars.

Some reports say Chinese pirates nailed their prisoners' feet to the deck. Then they beat them to death, cut them up, and ate them.

Ruthless rovers
The Gujarati rovers were the most feared pirates in the Indian Ocean. When they sailed the west coast of India they took their families with them.

If they captured someone who had no treasure, they thought the victim might have swallowed it. So they forced prisoners to swallow tamarind root to make them vomit up any jewels.

Earache
Pirate queen Ching Shih did not like her sailors to desert. If they were caught she had their ears sliced off and shown to the other sailors as a lesson.

But that was kind compared to what pirate Ned Low did when he captured a Nantucket whaling ship. He made her captain eat his own sliced-off ears, sprinkled with salt. Then he killed him.

Sew cruel
Dutch pirate Dirk Chivers captured two ships in 1695. Captain Sawbridge was one of those taken prisoner. Sawbridge was not happy. Sawbridge moaned . . . and moaned . . . and moaned. Chivers was so fed up with his moaning he took a sail needle and sewed up Sawbridge's mouth.

Pitiless pirates
Some Cuban pirates captured the English ship *Eliza Ann*. A woman called Lucretia Parker wrote to her brother to tell the tale of what happened to the crew . . .

First they took off all of the crew's clothes except their shirts and trousers. Then they attacked them with swords, knives and axes. They were as ferocious as cannibals. They ignored pleas for mercy as the crew begged the murderers to spare their lives. Our Captain Smith tried to win the pirates' pity by telling them of his wife and three small children. But he was pleading with monsters who have no human feelings. After receiving a heavy blow from an axe he snapped the cords he was bound with and, trying to escape, he was met by another of the ruffians who plunged a knife into his heart. I was standing near him at the time and was covered with his blood. On receiving the wound he gave a single groan and fell, lifeless, at my feet. Dear brother, I don't need to paint a picture of my feelings at that awful moment!

Luckily a British warship appeared before they could turn on Lucretia. The pirates abandoned the *Eliza Ann* and she was saved. They were arrested later in Jamaica.

Lucretia Parker identified them and had the pleasure of watching them hang.

Rotten rules

Pirates may seem lawless, but they often had their own rules: the Pirate Articles.

Just like proper laws, you had to obey or be punished.

Sometimes pirates captured a trading ship and gave the crew a choice …

SIGN THE PIRATE ARTICLES AND JOIN US, OR WE'LL USE YOU LIKE A SLAVE

Sometimes they killed anyone who refused to sign. These are the Pirate Articles. Would you sign them … or die?

Every man on the crew has an equal vote on their action and an equal share of food and drink on the ship. The Captain shall receive two persons' share of any treasure.

All men shall have an equal share of treasure. Any man who takes more than his share of gold or jewels or money shall be punished by marooning.

No person shall play cards or dice for money.

Lights and candles shall be put out at eight o'clock each night.

Each person must make sure his own pistol and cutlass are well kept and ready for use at all times.

No boy or woman shall be allowed on board the ship when she sails. Any man carrying a woman to sea shall suffer death.[3]

Any person who deserts the ship in a battle shall suffer death or marooning.

There shall be no fighting on board ship. All quarrels shall be settled on the shore with sword and cutlass.

No person shall talk of leaving the crew until everyone has shared at least a thousand pounds.

The ship's musicians shall be allowed to rest on Sundays.

BUT … there wasn't just ONE pirate code. The one above was written by Black Bart – other pirates had other rules.

3 But what about women pirates? This is an actual document – ask the writer!

☠ Pirate ships ☠

If you're going to be a pirate then you need to give your ship a terrifying name. You would NOT want to call your ship something sweet like *Blessing* ... but pirate Captain Brown did. Which is your favorite from these deadly days of the Caribbean pirates?

Ship   Pirate

1. Black Joke   Benito de Soto
2. Delight   Francis Spriggs
3. Flying Dragon   Edmund Condent
4. New York Revenge   William Kidd
5. Night Rambler   Captain Cooper
6. Queen Anne's Revenge   Blackbeard
7. Snap Dragon   Captain Goldsmith
8. Speedy Return   John Bowen
9. Sudden Death   Derdrake
10. Tiger   Sir Richard Grenville

Pirate losers

Not many pirates lived an exciting and happy life. Most of them were simple criminals with a rough life and an unhappy end.

Captain Hiram Breakes (born 1745)

Breakes was a Dutch sailor who fell in love with a woman called Mrs. Snyde. Soon afterwards Mr. Snyde died ... from poison. Breakes and Mrs. Snyde were tried. Mrs. Snyde said she didn't do it and they got away with murder.

Then Breakes stole his boss's ship and used it to attack a treasure ship from Chile. He had the crew murdered.

He said ...

> DEAD MEN TELL NO TALES

This was not a very clever thing to say. (Pirate Erik Cobham said pretty much the same thing, "Dead cats don't meow.")

When he went back to Holland he found that Mrs. Snyde had tried to poison their baby son and had been hanged. Breakes was so upset he threw himself off a Dutch dike and drowned himself.

You COULD say ... Snyde died; Mrs. Snyde tried; Mrs. Snyde lied; Baby Snyde died; Mrs. Snyde tried; Mrs. Snyde died; Breakes cried.

Abraham Cooke (1611–48)

This Welshman went to the Caribbean to herd cattle. He killed the cattle and sold the meat to the Spanish treasure ships. Then he discovered it was better to rob those ships.

He and his men stole so much treasure they built houses at Port Royal with doors of gold. Then Cooke sailed into a trap. He attacked a Spanish trading ship filled with Spanish soldiers and Cooke died in the fighting.

Cyril Hood (died 1648)

Cyril Hood was a useless buccaneer. In 1648 he gave up pirating and decided to make some money by betraying his old pirate pals.

Hood went to a Spanish captain and said, "I know where the next attack is planned – pay me one hundred gold pieces and I'll tell you." The Spanish captain didn't believe sad Cyril and refused to pay. So horrible Hood said, "All right, give me a bottle of rum and I'll tell you." This time the captain agreed. Cyril Hood betrayed buccaneer Abraham Cooke. Cooke got killed – Hood got drunk. Cooke's cousin Abel got hold of Hood and hanged him from the mast of his ship.

HE'S OVER THERE

Rachel Wall (1760–89)

Around the age of 16, blue-eyed Rachel took a trip to Pennsylvania for the funeral of her grandfather. While wandering the docks she met a shady fisherman by the name of George Wall. She soon married him, and the two of them went to live in Boston.

The hungry couple stole a ship and began pirating off the Isle of Shoals. They tricked passing ships by pretending to be in trouble. "Oh, help us!" pretty Rachel would cry. Once they had robbed their victims they would sink the captured ships and drown everyone aboard.

Then in 1782 George was washed away in a storm. Rachel made a living by creeping on board ships in the harbor and raiding the cabins. She was good at it. But in 1789 she was caught and tried. At the age of 29 she was hanged.

William Fly (died 1726)

Fly was a boxer before he joined a pirate ship. He led a mutiny and captured the captain. "Jump or we'll throw you overboard." The captain was thrown. Fly took over and was a pitiless master – he had many men lashed with a hundred lashes.

Fly was a hopeless sailor and managed to capture just one ship before his crew mutinied. They didn't throw him overboard. They handed him over for hanging.

At least Fly enjoyed his execution. He stood on the gallows, holding bunches of flowers, smiling and waving. The noose wasn't very well made so Fly tied the knot properly before slipping it over his head.

John Quelch (died 1704)

In 1703, John Quelch set off on the privateer *Charles*. He didn't like the captain much so, shortly after leaving the dock, Quelch tossed him overboard. He headed for the south Atlantic, as a privateer to rob French and Spanish ships.

Not long afterwards he came across a Portuguese gold ship and robbed her. Big mistake. England was at peace with Portugal and was not allowed to attack their ships.

The English Navy wanted to show Portugal how sorry they were. Quelch was captured, taken back to Maine, and hanged.

Nicholas Brown (died 1726)

In the 1700s, Brown was a pirate attacking ships around Jamaica. He was caught and sentenced to hang. But the King spared his life if he promised to give up piracy.

Brown, however, did go back to piracy and became known as "The Grand Pirate." Now the British Navy set out to hunt him down. The man who caught Brown was his old school pal, John Drudge. In 1726, Drudge killed Brown … then chopped off his head and pickled it. He took the head back to Britain to claim the reward.

Rahmah bin Jabr (1756–1826)

Rahmah made himself the most famous pirate of the Persian Gulf. He started off badly, losing one eye in a battle, but he raided ships for 50 years and lived to the age of 70.

This piratical pensioner should have stopped there and lived to 80. But he upset the people of Bahrain so much they sent all of their navy after him. Rahmah knew he was beaten. He let his enemies close in on him. Then he set fire to the gunpowder store on his own ship. He blew up many enemy ships … the bits of bin Jabr must have enjoyed that.

Manuel Pardal Rivero (died 1670)

Manuel was from Portugal but became a privateer for Spain. The trouble was he wasn't a very good pirate. In his first raid he sailed for the English fleet in Jamaica … but the wind changed and he attacked Grand Cayman instead. He landed at a poor village, stole two boats, captured four children, and sailed off.

He finally reached Jamaica and called the governor, Sir Henry Morgan, to come out and fight. Morgan sailed off and attacked Panama instead and Manuel couldn't stop him. At last he did meet the English ship of Captain John Morris. Manuel's crew jumped overboard – they drowned or were shot as they swam ashore. Sir Henry Morgan chased Manuel along the beach and shot him dead.

Captain William Kidd (1645–1701)

In 1696 Captain Kidd was sent to the Indian Ocean with the job of catching pirates. Rich men in America gave him the money to buy a ship. But those men hoped he would really be robbing and bringing them back a fortune.

Kidd did capture a rich prize, the *Quedah Merchant*, but decided to share most of his loot with his crew instead. He hid the rest on an island. The rich Americans were furious. When he returned he was arrested and found guilty of piracy. He was sent back to England to hang.

He was hanged twice – the rope broke the first time. Then he was hanged in chains till his body rotted. Kidd died. His rich "friends" lived on.

And one pirate winner …

Red Legs Greaves c. 1670–80

Red Legs Greaves was from a Scottish slave family. He escaped and joined the cruel Captain Hawkins as a Caribbean pirate. But Red Legs refused to torture or kill prisoners. His bare Scottish legs burned in the sun and that's how he got his name.

Red Legs made a fortune in one raid on a Spanish fortress. He retired to Nevis Island but was betrayed and arrested and sentenced to hang. Then an earthquake on Nevis destroyed the jail and Red Legs was one of the few who lived. Lucky Red Legs.

Kindly Red Legs turned pirate hunter and was given a pardon. He died of old age, very rich and loved by many people. Maybe the kindly pirate deserved his good luck.

JO-HO-HO

Talk like a pirate

If a pirate shouted at you ...

Would you know what he was talking about? Probably not. Here are ten words to help you ...

HEAVE TO

Want a ship to stop? Then call out "heave to" because that means "stand still." It has nothing to do with "heaving overboard" … which is what you'd do if you found an enemy on your ship….

I CAN'T SWIM! I'LL DROWN

DON'T WORRY— THE SHARKS WILL EAT YOU LONG BEFORE THAT!

That dried fish may not look very tasty but it's better than nothing. Just remember you're eating something pirates call Hairy Willy.

HAIRY WILLY

SLOPS

"Slops" was the 1700s sailor word for trousers. Sailors were among the first people to wear trousers. Some went down to the ankles, some just below the knees.

A "lubber" is a clumsy person on a ship. He'd be happier on land. If you really want a cutlass up your nose, then call a pirate a "landlubber."

LANDLUBBER

SCUTTLE

If you are in danger from attack by another ship then you may want to sink your own ship and row off in a lifeboat. Do NOT say, "Poke a little hole in my boat and let it sink." To sink your own ship is to "scuttle" it.

If you see a ship you want to capture you have to tell it to stop. Do NOT shout, "Excuse me, but would you mind slowing down so I can rob you?" Shout "Avast ye!" It means "Stop ... or else!"

AVAST YE

SHIVER ME TIMBERS

If a ship gets a sudden blast from a cannon, then its masts ("timbers") are shaken (or "shivered"). So a shocked ship has shivered timbers. If YOU get a shock then don't say, "Goodness me, I am surprised!", say, "Shiver me timbers!"

The very bottom of the ship. This is where water seeps in, rats live, and all the filth of the ship ends up. It stinks, and the air down there is deadly. Never call a pirate a bilge rat or he may take a cutlass to your cheeky tongue.

BILGE

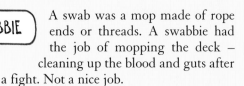

SWABBIE

A swab was a mop made of rope ends or threads. A swabbie had the job of mopping the deck – cleaning up the blood and guts after a fight. Not a nice job.

Scurvy was a disease that many sailors suffered from at sea. Your skin went scabby and even your mom wouldn't want to kiss you! And a "knave" is a villain. So scurvy knave or scabby villain: Take your pick – or pick your scab.

But most of all … talk tough.
Whatever you say, make it sound nasty. A pirate told his prisoner, Captain William Snelgrave, in the 1700s …

> *I will give you this warning … never argue with a pirate. For, suppose I had chopped your skull in two for your cheek, what would you have got? Nothing but destruction …*

Fly the flags

If you want to be a pirate, then get a flag. Every pirate crew had its own flag – usually with skeletons, skulls, bones, and swords.

The pirate flag was often called the "Jolly Roger" – that is from the French "jolie rouge" or "pretty red."

The first pirate flags were red. The other name for the pirate flag was:

Captain Death

The black flag may have been a signal that meant …

GIVE UP AND WE WILL LET YOU LIVE

If the victim tried to escape, then the red flag was raised. That meant …

OK, CHAPS, WE'RE GOING TO KILL YOU

Here are a few of Captain Death's jolly flags:

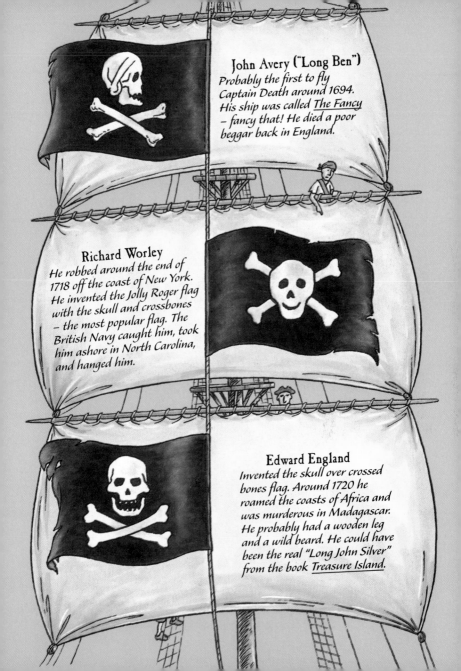

John Avery ("Long Ben")
*Probably the first to fly
Captain Death around 1694.
His ship was called <u>The Fancy</u>
– fancy that! He died a poor
beggar back in England.*

Richard Worley
*He robbed around the end of
1718 off the coast of New York.
He invented the Jolly Roger flag
with the skull and crossbones
– the most popular flag. The
British Navy caught him, took
him ashore in North Carolina,
and hanged him.*

Edward England
*Invented the skull over crossed
bones flag. Around 1720 he
roamed the coasts of Africa and
was murderous in Madagascar.
He probably had a wooden leg
and a wild beard. He could have
been the real "Long John Silver"
from the book <u>Treasure Island</u>.*

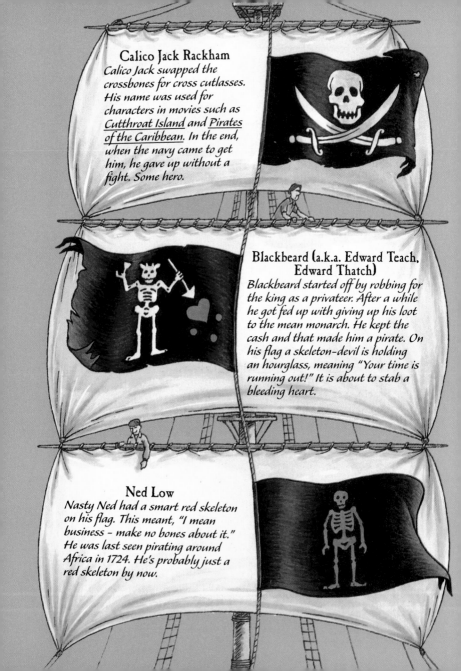

Calico Jack Rackham
Calico Jack swapped the crossbones for cross cutlasses. His name was used for characters in movies such as <u>Cutthroat Island</u> and <u>Pirates of the Caribbean</u>. In the end, when the navy came to get him, he gave up without a fight. Some hero.

Blackbeard (a.k.a. Edward Teach, Edward Thatch)
Blackbeard started off by robbing for the king as a privateer. After a while he got fed up with giving up his loot to the mean monarch. He kept the cash and that made him a pirate. On his flag a skeleton-devil is holding an hourglass, meaning "Your time is running out!" It is about to stab a bleeding heart.

Ned Low
Nasty Ned had a smart red skeleton on his flag. This meant, "I mean business - make no bones about it." He was last seen pirating around Africa in 1724. He's probably just a red skeleton by now.

Black Bart

Black Bart (Bartholomew Roberts) hated the governors of Barbados and Martinique. So he had their heads put on his flag as a warning ... Black Barty designed a flag, portraying a giant figure of himself standing, sword in hand, astride two skulls labeled A.B.H. ("Barbadian's head") and A.M.H. ("a Martinican's head").

Note: Never mind how much you hate the school principals, don't try this at school ... or at skull.

Thomas Tew

His Captain Death was a simple message ... "This is what you're going to get if you don't give up quietly." This flag was seen everywhere, from America to the Mediterranean in Europe. But the cutlass didn't save him when a cannon shot blew him to pieces.

Emanuel Wynne

This French pirate copied the rest. The skull, the crossbones, AND the hourglass. You may notice the hourglass is full at both ends – it will never run out. Maybe the message was, "If you don't give up, then I warn you, you'll die of old age!"

Christopher Moody

Christopher Moody attacked ships off the coast of the Carolinas between 1713 and 1718. He may not be famous as a pirate but he is remembered for his colorful flag.

Henry Morgan

The most horrible flag, to the Spanish, was this one. It is the Union Jack, flown by British ships from 1606 to 1801. When Britain was at war with Spain, privateers like Henry Morgan flew it as they attacked Spanish galleons. Naughty Morgan even attacked the Spanish when Britain was at PEACE with them! Well, a privateer has to make a living.

WARNING:

SOME of these flags may have been invented in pirate tales. Not many pirate flags have been found. MOST of these could be fake or made up by writers.

Foul facts

1. Pirates were often at sea for a long time, so they took hens along (for eggs and meat). They also took "hardtack" biscuits and limes. Their meat was often full of maggots and their biscuits were alive with weevils. They brushed some off and swallowed the rest.

2. On one island pirates were short of food so they had to eat snakes and monkeys.

3. When they needed to go to the bathroom they used a rope cage hanging over the sea.

4. When pirates buried treasure they would sometimes murder a prisoner and bury him on top of the treasure. That way the prisoner's ghost would guard the treasure. A sort of spook-curity guard. If they didn't have a prisoner then they might kill a member of the crew.

There was a sensible reason for this too. If the law came looking for the treasure they would say …

A FRESH PILE OF EARTH, THEIR TREASURE IS THERE!

But when they dug down, they would say …

NO, IT'S JUST A GRAVE. FILL IT IN AGAIN

5. Not many pirate ships had a doctor on board. So who cut off your leg or your arm if it was shattered in battle?

The carpenter, of course, because he was handy with the saw.

Or sometimes it would be the ship's cook, who was good at carving up meat. That's neat.

Captain Ned Low enjoyed torturing his victims. But in one drunken attack he tangled with one of his own men and had his cheek slashed open.

The drunken ship's doctor tried to sew it up but Low didn't like it and told the doctor:

YOU COULDN'T SEW A BUTTON ON A SHIRT, YOU IDIOT!

FINE – SEE IF YOU CAN DO BETTER!

Low killed the doctor, then did just what he said … sewed up his own face. It left a scary scar. Just what a pirate wanted!

6. There were usually more rats on a ship than sailors.

Rats chewed the ropes, they chewed the wood, and they even chewed the pirates. They also ate the food stored in the cabins.

Pirates would sometimes have rat hunts. One Spanish ship sailed from Europe to South America and had rat hunts along the way. The captain reported …

We killed 4,000 rats on that one journey.

7. Pirates kept pets. They liked to take monkeys because they could sell them when they landed in Europe.

8. Pirates also kept working animals. Buccaneers kept dogs to help them with their hunting. Many ships carried cats. But the crew were very superstitious. Here are the rules …

1. If a black cat walks towards a sailor, he will be lucky.

2. If a black cat walks towards a sailor but then turns around and walks away, he will be unlucky.

3. If a black cat is thrown overboard, a storm will follow and the ship will be cursed.

9. The captain was in charge of the ship and you had to obey him in a battle. But when the crew were not fighting they could vote to have a new captain.

A "good" pirate captain was one who helped his crew win lots of treasure.

A "bad" pirate captain was usually a dead pirate captain.

OUR CAPTAIN IS HOPELESS

10. The worst job on a pirate ship was the job of "powder monkey." In a battle the powder monkey had to keep the gunners supplied with gunpowder. The job was usually given to boys about eleven or twelve years old – too young to fight with swords and pistols.

They were often kidnapped from their parents and forced to work. They were the youngest on the ship and the most bullied.

Powder monkey misery.

Pirate punishments

It was all very well being a pirate – roaming the seas and bashing people – until you were caught. Then you were treated with little pity.

HANGING

Pirates who were caught were usually hanged. In the 1700s this was a slow and horrible way to die.

In London the hangings didn't take place at the usual jails. The pirates were hanged at the docks where sailors could watch and cheer … or fear. The place was known as Execution Dock.

When the tide came in the bodies went under the water. After three soakings they were cut down.

Pirates were afraid of being hanged. If they were not given a proper burial they thought their spirits would go to hell. So some chose to die rather than be captured.

Two of Ned Low's pirates were terrified when a navy ship chased them. But they could not kill themselves – that was against their religion too. They would go to hell!

So each agreed to stand toe to toe, put a pistol to his friend's head, and each would kill the other.

The ship escaped just in time. That saved someone having to mop brains off the deck.

HANGING IN CHAINS

The pirate's dead body would often be left swinging in the wind to teach people a lesson.

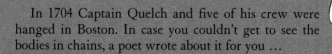

In 1704 Captain Quelch and five of his crew were hanged in Boston. In case you couldn't get to see the bodies in chains, a poet wrote about it for you …

> You pirates who against God's laws did fight,
> Have all been hanged, which is very right,
> Some of you were old and some were young,
> And on the Boston gallows they were hung.

Captain Kidd's dead body was painted with tar so it wouldn't rot. The black corpse was hung in a cage by the River Thames.

🦴 DID YOU KNOW…? 🦴

If a pirate was captured he would usually be taken to the nearest port for hanging. But he wasn't given a comfortable trip. Sometimes he'd be bound with ropes, then hung up with the sails to swing in the wind.

BURIED FACEDOWN

The executed pirate was often buried on the seashore near where he was executed.

He wasn't buried in a churchyard because then his spirit would go to heaven.

Just to be extra sure his spirit stayed lost forever, he was buried facedown.

BURNED AT THE STAKE

Pirates in North Africa often captured Arab prisoners. The pirates were Christians (sort of) while the Arabs were Muslims. So the pirates forced the Arab Muslims to become Arab Christians ... or die.

The trouble was the Muslims hated the Arab Christians more than anything. If one was captured by his old Arab friends he faced an extra-nasty punishment ... he was burned alive.

BURIED ALIVE

Pirates lived by the sea and some died by the sea.

Welsh pirate Colyn Dolphyn was trapped at St. Donats on the south coast of Wales. He was buried in the sand up to his neck. The tide came in slowly and he drowned.

WATER WAY TO GO

DRY IN THE SUN

At Dead Man's Cay, near Kingston, Jamaica, pirates were executed by being fastened in an iron cage and hung up on a post to "dry in the sun."

Of course, after a slow and painful day they would "die in the sun."

The cage was made to fit tight around the pirate so his bones wouldn't fall away when his flesh rotted. Skeletons could hang there for years.

A REAL DRAG

One popular sort of punishment was to drag a pirate along behind a ship on a length of rope until he begged for mercy, drowned, or was eaten by sharks. (A lot of people PAY to have this done to them today. They call it water-skiing.)

A THOUSAND CUTS

The Chinese had the most vicious punishment for pirate Nicholas Iquan. It was a slow death, called the "death of a thousand cuts":

• A knife made a cut in the flesh, then the wound was sealed with a hot iron.

• This was done hundreds of times, working from the hands and feet towards the heart.

Just to make it worse for Iquan he had to watch this execution carried out on his two sons.

GRUB UP

A pirate prisoner held below deck on a pirate ship could be offered some disgusting food – grubs, beetles, or cockroaches. They would have some slimy water to wash them down with. It was either eat the grubby grub or starve.

BOLT UP

An odd punishment for a pirate was to have iron bolts jammed into his mouth.

Dire deaths

Pirates didn't belong to any country. So any country could capture a pirate crew and punish them. If you were lucky they took away your ship. If you were unlucky you met a nastier end ...

Caesar's pirates

Around 75 BC young Julius Caesar was on his way to Rhodes when the ship he was on was captured by pirates. The pirates said they'd set him free if his family paid 20 talents (gold pieces).

Julius was upset ...

I'M GOING TO BE AN EMPEROR, I'M WORTH MORE THAN THAT. ASK FOR AT LEAST 50 TALENTS.

So the pirates asked his parents for 50 and got it. He was set free.

Big mistake.

Years later Caesar hunted them down and had them all crucified.

He was a little cross – but they got a great big cross.

Benito de Soto

Ruthless de Soto was caught in Gibraltar and sentenced to hang in 1832.

He was sent off to Cadiz to be hanged along with his crew. He arrived in Cadiz along with his coffin. A gallows was built on one of the docks and the death was a cruel one.

The pirate was brought to the gallows on a donkey cart and had to sit on his own coffin. When he reached the gallows, he had the noose put around his neck and the cart would pull away leaving the pirate to strangle slowly. De Soto did not want to die that way. He stood on top of his coffin, reached for the rope and put the noose around his neck. He smiled to the crowd and cried:

You don't need me to tell you what that means.

You do? Oh, very well, it means, "So long everybody!"

He jumped from the cart to his death. It was still slow and painful – but at least he went in style.

Black Bart

Bart was probably the cleverest pirate ever to set sail. He captured over 400 ships and took £50,000,000 in loot. He was killed in 1722 during a battle with an English warship off the coast of Africa. Half his throat was torn away by a cannon blast. His crew dumped his body overboard so that he would not be taken prisoner, alive or dead.

There were 254 people on his ship, including 70 African slaves and 18 French sailors, all of whom he had forced into piracy. They may have been glad to see him dead … but not for long. After the defeat 52 were hanged.

Bart's motto was …

> A SHORT LIFE BUT A MERRY ONE

Thomas Tew

Thomas Tew roamed across the Atlantic, Mediterranean, and even the Red Sea.

His end came around 1695 during a sea battle with an Indian ship. An enemy cannon fired small pieces of metal at his ship – not the usual cannonballs. These shredded Tew's belly and his guts started to fall out onto the deck. He lay screaming in agony. His crew became so terrified by the sight that they gave up without another shot being fired.

William Lewis

In 1727 Lewis was chasing a rich treasure ship and it was getting away from him. He climbed the mast and began to tear out his own hair. He screamed …

> *Good devil – take this until we meet in hell!*

Sure enough his ship sped up and caught the treasure ship.

But Lewis's crew were terrified. "He has made a deal with the Devil – the Devil will take him … and then he'll come for us!"

They decided that Lewis had to die.

That night they crept into his cabin and stabbed him to death. He went to hell sooner than he thought.

🕱 DID YOU KNOW...? 🕱

Eustace was a Dutch monk in the 1200s. He gave up God and made a deal with the Devil (they said). The Devil gave Eustace the power to make his ship invisible.

It didn't do Eustace much good. He was beaten in a sea battle in 1217 and his head was cut off.

BEHOLD THE HEAD OF A PIRATE – I THINK

Captain George Lowther

In 1722, Lowther pulled his ship, *Happy Delivery*, up onto a beach to scrape the bottom clean. A navy ship came along and Lowther's crew were trapped on the island, Blanquilla, near Venezuela.

Lowther jumped through a cabin window and ran off to hide on the deserted island.

But he couldn't last long with no food or water. At last the navy found his corpse.

There was an empty pistol in its hand and a bullet through its brain.

Captain Morgan

Sir Henry Morgan gave up pirating and became governor of Jamaica in 1674. But he was bored and drank endless glasses of rum to pass the time. This destroyed his liver and, as he lay dying, Morgan swelled like a balloon and turned yellow.

The doctor only knew one cure – he had Morgan covered from head to toe in wet mud.

It didn't work. Morgan died, brown and sticky.

Blackbeard

In 1718, Lieutenant Maynard of HMS *Pearl* was sent to hunt Blackbeard down.

Maynard hid his men below deck and Blackbeard jumped aboard to kill him. That's when Maynard's force leaped out of their hiding places.

Maynard killed Blackbeard in a famous hand-to-hand fight. It's said that Blackbeard was shot five times and stabbed another 20 times before he finally fell. His head was cut off and stuck on the mast.

His body was thrown overboard and it was said that the headless corpse swam around the ship three times before it sank.

✖ DID YOU KNOW...? ✖

Blackbeard fell in love with 16-year-old Mary Ormond and made her his fourteenth wife. (He was a popular man.) He sailed off in 1618 and left her in Portsmouth. He never returned. (He couldn't. He was dead.) They say her ghost wanders the cliff tops looking for his ship.

Caesar

Nothing to do with Julius Caesar! This Caesar was an African slave who ran away and joined Blackbeard's crew in the Caribbean.

He was one of the few men Blackbeard really trusted and he was given an order …

I DO NOT WANT TO BE HANGED. IF I AM EVER IN DANGER, THEN BLOW UP THE SHIP AND SEND ME TO A WATERY GRAVE.

I WILL, CAPTAIN

When Blackbeard was shot and stabbed in 1718, Caesar hurried to blow up the ship as he promised. But two of his pirate shipmates stopped him.

Caesar was caught and hanged along with the others.

William Duell – who didn't die a pirate death:
Duell was hanged in 1740 at Newgate Prison in London. His body was cut down and taken to the doctors to be cut up. (They wanted to experiment to see how the human body worked.)

This was an extra punishment that pirates feared – they believed they couldn't go to heaven in bits.

The doctors washed Duell's body and got ready to start carving … then noticed he was still breathing. Two hours later he was sitting in a chair. He was sent back to Newgate Prison, then transported to America.

> ### 🕱 DID YOU KNOW…? 🕱
> A ghastly tale is told of a ghostly pirate ship. Late one night in October, 1864, a US ship was ready to set sail. Louis Billings, the master of the small ship, was getting ready to raise the anchor when he was frightened by a shriek from one of the crew. He reported …

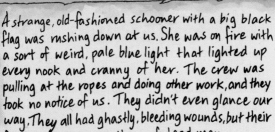

A strange, old-fashioned schooner with a big black flag was rushing down at us. She was on fire with a sort of weird, pale blue light that lighted up every nook and cranny of her. The crew was pulling at the ropes and doing other work, and they took no notice of us. They didn't even glance our way. They all had ghastly, bleeding wounds, but their faces and eyes were those of dead men.

The man who had screamed had fallen to his knees, his teeth chattering as he gasped out a prayer. I rushed forward, and told the crew to start saying any prayer they knew. Suddenly the schooner vanished before my eyes.

Some say that it was the ghost of Jean Lafitte's pirate ship, The Pride, that sank off Galveston Island in 1821 or 1822.

You may think it was a bad dream or a lie. But that same ship was seen again in 1892, in the same place, with the same crew.

Epilogue

Pirates seem so much fun. People like to play at being pirates, dress like pirates, and tell stories of pirates.

They have been doing this for hundreds of years.

Some of the stories written about pirates have been believed by many people.

Take the story of Jose Gaspar. This is how the story goes. You have to decide. Is it true... or is it a lie?

- Jose Gaspar was born in Spain in 1756. He became a captain for King Charles III but a Spanish princess fell in love with him. He turned her down so she tried to have him arrested.

- He fled to America in his ship <u>Floridablanco</u> and turned pirate. He captured over 400 ships in the next 30 years. In 1821 he was ready to retire but was attacked by the USS <u>Enterprise</u>.[4]

4 That is the "*United States Ship Enterprise*," not the *Starship Enterprise* from *Star Trek* which hadn't been built in 1821 and which STILL hasn't been built ... but you know it WILL be because you've seen the movies!

He knew it was all over so he wrapped an anchor chain around his waist and jumped to his death.

◆ His crew buried his $30 million treasure near Peace River, and most of it is still there today.

◆ Every year there is a Gaspar Pirate Festival in Florida and tourists love it. There is even a statue of the pirate.

So he MUST be true.

BUT ... there was

- no Captain Gaspar in the Spanish Navy
- no ship called *Floridablanco*
- no record of the US Navy attacking a ship of that name.

It is almost certainly a lie.

Pirates make great stories. But the truth is they were cruel and stupid men and women who lived and died miserable lives.

Truly horrible history.

Interesting Index

Hang on! This isn't one of your boring old indexes. This is the only index in the world where you will find "vomiting cows," "mopping-up brains," "pickled heads," and all the other things you really HAVE to know if you want to be a horrible historian. Read it and creep.